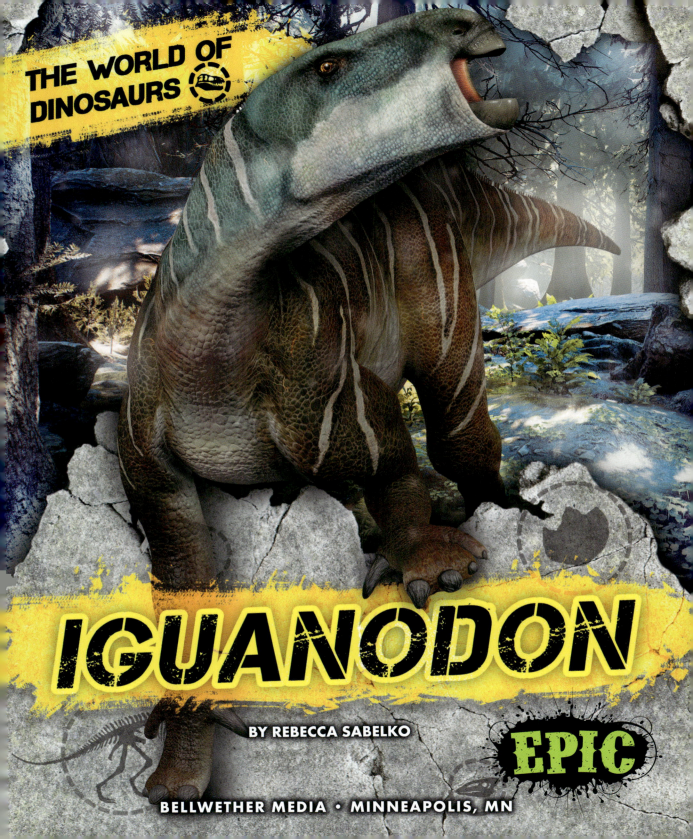

EPIC

EPIC BOOKS are no ordinary books. They burst with intense action, high-speed heroics, and shadows of the unknown. Are you ready for an Epic adventure?

This edition first published in 2021 by Bellwether Media, Inc.

No part of this publication may be reproduced in whole or in part without written permission of the publisher. For information regarding permission, write to Bellwether Media, Inc., Attention: Permissions Department, 6012 Blue Circle Drive, Minnetonka, MN 55343.

Library of Congress Cataloging-in-Publication Data

LC record for Iguanodon available at https://lccn.loc.gov/2020048059

Text copyright © 2021 by Bellwether Media, Inc. EPIC and associated logos are trademarks and/or registered trademarks of Bellwether Media, Inc.

Editor: Betsy Rathburn   Designer: Jeffrey Kollock

Printed in the United States of America, North Mankato, MN.

TABLE OF CONTENTS

THE WORLD OF THE IGUANODON	4
WHAT WAS THE IGUANODON?	6
DIET AND DEFENSES	10
FOSSILS AND EXTINCTION	16
GET TO KNOW THE IGUANODON	20
GLOSSARY	22
TO LEARN MORE	23
INDEX	24

THE WORLD OF THE IGUANODON

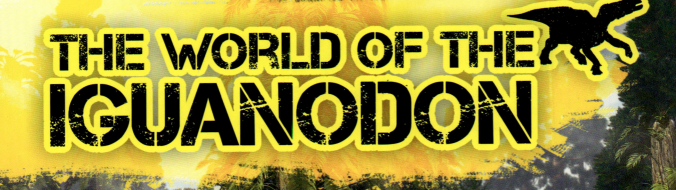

The iguanodon was one of the first dinosaurs ever studied!

It lived around 140 million years ago during the Early **Cretaceous period**. This was the last period of the **Mesozoic era**.

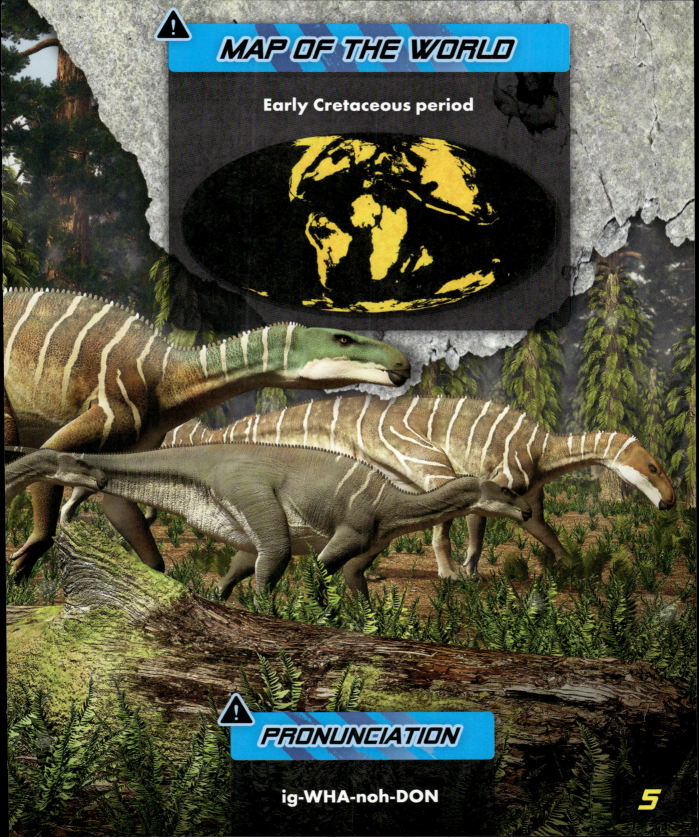

MAP OF THE WORLD

Early Cretaceous period

PRONUNCIATION

ig-WHA-noh-DON

5

WHAT WAS THE IGUANODON?

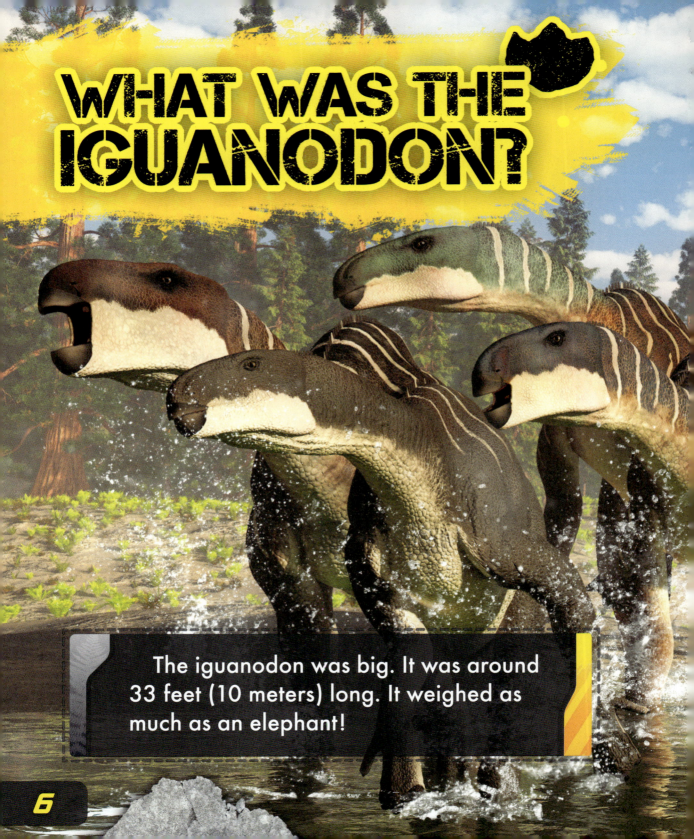

The iguanodon was big. It was around 33 feet (10 meters) long. It weighed as much as an elephant!

It mostly walked on four legs. But it could also walk on its longer back legs.

NAME GAME

The word *iguanodon* means "iguana tooth."

SIZE CHART

15 feet (4.6 meters)
10 feet (3 meters)
5 feet (1.5 meters)

7

The iguanodon had unusual front feet. Each foot had five toes. One toe was a spiked thumb.

HORN OR THUMB?

Scientists once thought the iguanodon's thumb spike was a horn!

spiked thumb

The three middle toes formed hooflike claws. These helped the dinosaur walk.

DIET AND DEFENSES

IGUANODON DIET

leafy plants

ferns

tree leaves

10

The iguanodon was an **herbivore**. It mostly ate ground plants.

It also ate from trees. It stood on its back legs. Its thumbs likely pulled leaves from branches. The thumbs may have also opened fruits or nuts!

The dinosaur snapped tough plants with its hard beak.

beak

Its jaws were filled with bumpy teeth. The teeth worked like scissors to cut plants.

This dinosaur had many **predators**. It lived in a **herd** to stay safe.

herd

RUN AWAY!

The iguanodon may have run from its enemies. It could run around 12 miles (19.3 kilometers) per hour!

But sometimes enemies got too close. The iguanodon may have jabbed at enemies with its sharp thumbs!

FOSSILS AND EXTINCTION

The iguanodon went **extinct** around 110 million years ago.

Many scientists believe later **duck-billed** dinosaurs are related to the iguanodon.

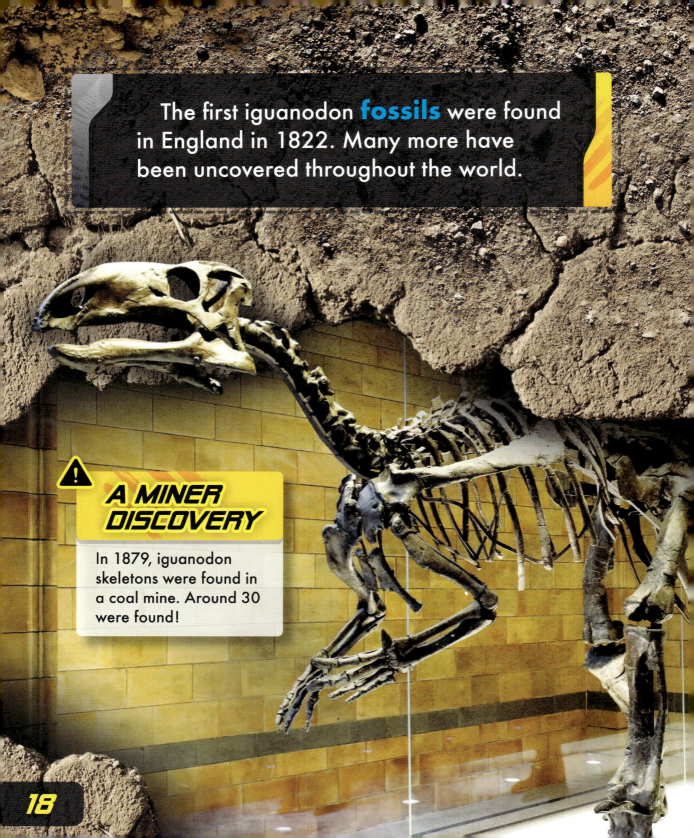

The first iguanodon **fossils** were found in England in 1822. Many more have been uncovered throughout the world.

A MINER DISCOVERY

In 1879, iguanodon skeletons were found in a coal mine. Around 30 were found!

IGUANODON FOSSIL MAP

KEY
○ fossil site

Fossils have taught us a lot about how this dinosaur lived. But there is still so much more to discover!

GET TO KNOW THE IGUANODON

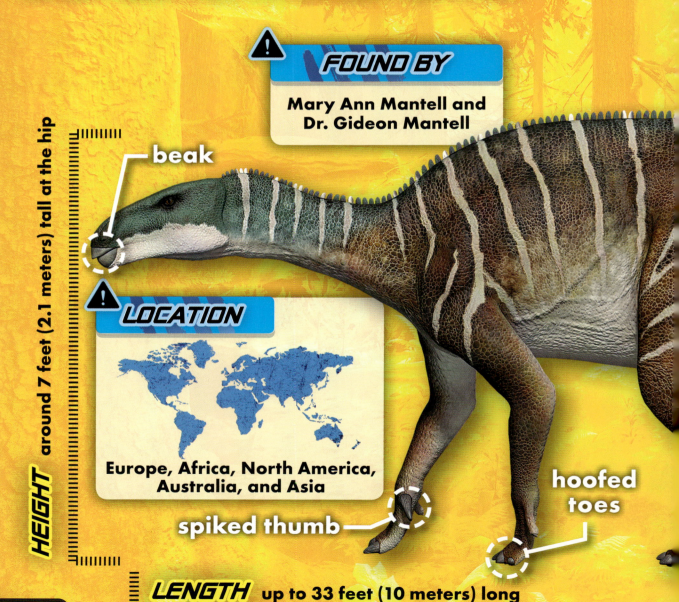

FOUND BY
Mary Ann Mantell and Dr. Gideon Mantell

beak

LOCATION
Europe, Africa, North America, Australia, and Asia

spiked thumb

hoofed toes

HEIGHT around 7 feet (2.1 meters) tall at the hip

LENGTH up to 33 feet (10 meters) long

20

ERA

140 million to 110 million years ago during the Early Cretaceous period

FIRST FOSSILS FOUND

Sussex, England, in 1822

FOOD

ferns, leafy plants

WEIGHT

up to 10,000 pounds (4,536 kilograms)

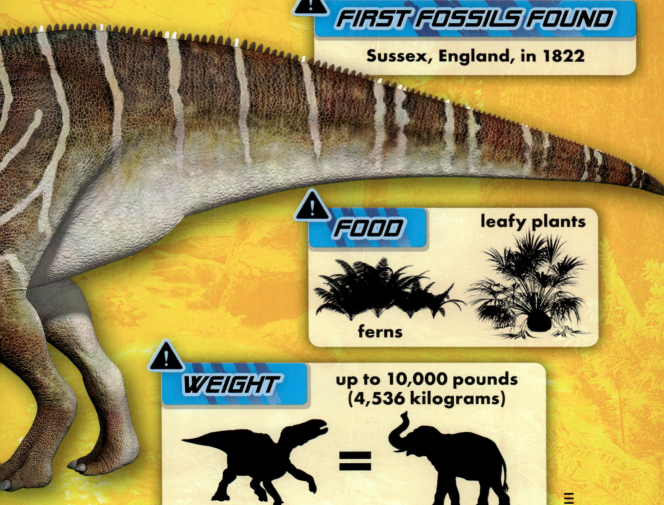

21

GLOSSARY

Cretaceous period—the last period of the Mesozoic era that occurred between 145 million and 66 million years ago; the Early Cretaceous period lasted from 145 million years ago to around 100 million years ago.

duck-billed—related to types of dinosaurs from the Late Cretaceous period that often had beaks, crests on their heads, and jaws filled with grinding teeth

extinct—no longer living

fossils—the remains of living things that lived long ago

herbivore—an animal that only eats plants

herd—a group of dinosaurs that lived and traveled together

Mesozoic era—a time in history in which dinosaurs lived on Earth; the first birds, mammals, and flowering plants appeared on Earth during the Mesozoic era.

predators—animals that hunt other animals for food

TO LEARN MORE

AT THE LIBRARY

Braun, Eric. *Could You Survive the Cretaceous Period?: An Interactive Prehistoric Adventure*. North Mankato, Minn.: Capstone Press, 2020.

Radley, Gail. *Iguanodon*. Mankato, Minn.: Black Rabbit Books, 2021.

Sabelko, Rebecca. *Parasaurolophus*. Minneapolis, Minn.: Bellwether Media, 2021.

ON THE WEB

Factsurfer.com gives you a safe, fun way to find more information.

1. Go to www.factsurfer.com.

2. Enter "iguanodon" into the search box and click 🔍.

3. Select your book cover to see a list of related content.

INDEX

beak, 12
claws, 9
duck-billed dinosaurs, 17
Early Cretaceous period, 4, 5
England, 18
extinct, 16
feet, 8
food, 10, 11, 12, 13
fossils, 18, 19
get to know, 20-21
herbivore, 11
herd, 14
jaws, 13
legs, 7, 11

map, 5, 19
Mesozoic era, 4
name, 7
predators, 14, 15
pronunciation, 5
scientists, 17
size, 6, 7
skeletons, 18
speed, 14
teeth, 13
thumb, 8, 11, 15
toes, 8, 9
walk, 7, 9

The images in this book are reproduced through the courtesy of: James Kuether, front cover, pp. 1, 4-5, 6-7, 8-9, 10-11, 12-13, 14-15, 16-17, 20-21; bryan/ Wikipedia, pp. 18, 19